# 101 Tips for Creating Prosperity and Abundance for Professional Women

Ted A. Moreno and June Davidson

Copyright © 2015 Ted A. Moreno and June Davidson

All rights reserved.

ISBN:978-1512154849

# ACKNOWLEDGMENTS

I'd like to acknowledge June Davidson for her invaluable partnership in the writing of this book. I'd also like to thank Dian Anderson and the Coachtastics. Special thanks to my wife Natalie. In addition, thank you to Craig Valine, Christie Wright, and Michele Guzy.

*Ted A. Moreno*

I would like to acknowledge my partner Dian Anderson, for her many years of continued support and awareness as I live and create in the "Juniverse". I love when we take the time to celebrate with champagne.

Big Thank Yous:

To my sister, Bess Bowman, who gives me unconditional support even when I'm lost in my creations.

To my niece, Karen Bowman, who gives me unconditional support in the Juniverse.

To my brother, Bill, to whom I am so connected with a depth of understanding.

*June Davidson*

# Introduction

Most people want to be successful in life. They will tell you that they want the good things that life offers such as money, nice things, leisure time and fun.

The question is: what is success? Success usually means different things to different people.

A good definition of success is the **progressive realization of worthwhile personal goals.** If you set goals and take the consistent action to begin achieving them, then you are a success.

Success comes in all different shapes and sizes with one common denominator. Success is important and it takes work to become successful.

The following 101 Tips are for the professional woman who has the goal of creating greater prosperity and abundance. It's for those women who are ready to release old patterns of thinking and behavior about money that no longer serve them. These tips will help you begin to think differently about money, give you some tools to use, and provide guidance on your way to attracting success, wealth and happiness.

Whatever prosperity and abundance means to you and whatever your financial goals are, you have the ability to achieve them. Start reading with that powerful belief firmly in place inside of you.

## 1. Realize Your Potential

In order to succeed at anything, you need to believe that you have the potential to reach your goals. For example, if you want increase your earning ability at your job or business, but lack the additional training or advanced knowledge to do so, achieving this goal is unlikely. However, if you are willing to invest in furthering your education, you can gain confidence in your potential and this will allow you to take steps needed to increase your earning power.

> *In knowing how to overcome little things, a centimeter at a time, gradually when bigger things come, you're prepared!*
>
> Katherine Dunham

## 2. Don't Look Back

Everyone has had money failures or has made financial mistakes in their past. To attract greater wealth, you must learn from those mistakes and see the value in these difficult lessons. Beating yourself up for past failures keeps you stuck in the past and is a waste of your energy. Choose to move forward and make better, more educated decisions from the lessons learned.

> *The art of life is not controlling what happens to us, but using what happens to us.*
>
> Gloria Steinham

3.    **Dare to Dream**

To increase your level of prosperity and abundance, you need to have goals, dreams and aspirations. Be honest with yourself as to what you want out of life and what you want to give of your life. Allow your mind to dream and think big. Imagine what it would be like if you could not fail. Most people ask for little, so they receive little.

> *When you have a dream you've got to grab it and never let go.*
> 
> Carol Burnett

4.    **Create a Plan**

No one plans to fail, people simply fail to plan. You may need to analyze your current situation first. To get where you want to go, you first need to know where you are. Then, write down your goals, short term and long term. Create timelines and benchmarks. Get clear about what is required for you to achieve your goals. Prepare for any obstacles than can come up. Read your goals regularly and revise when and if you need to.

> *You have to choose what you want to be. You have to choose your own path in life.*
> 
> Lailah Gifty Akita

5. **Don't Give Up**

To reach success, you must persevere. Distance swimmer Diana Nyad, at age 28, attempted to swim from Cuba to Florida and failed. In 2011, thirty three years later, she failed in her second attempt due to strong currents, pain and asthma. In 2011, her third attempt failed as well because of jellyfish stings, as did her fourth attempt in 2012 because of stings and storms. In 2013, at age 64, she became the first person to swim from Havana Cuba to Key West Florida without a shark cage. Keep striving even when it becomes challenging.

> *All of us suffer difficulties in our lives. And if you say to yourself 'find a way,' you'll make it through.*
> 
> Diana Nyad

6. **Have an Unstoppable Attitude**

You need to have determination and perseverance to achieve your financial goals. Close friends or family members, however, may feel it would be better if you focused your attention in another endeavor or business. Develop clear intent, along with an unstoppable attitude, then be determined to take action to succeed.

> *Courage doesn't always roar. Sometimes courage is the little voice at the end of the day that says I'll try again tomorrow.*
> 
> Mary Anne Radmacher

## 7. Stop Complaining

There is a correlation between complaining and a lack of financial success. Complaining about the obstacles you are facing is investing time and energy in what you don't want, and robbing you of the focus and energy you need to see opportunities for growth and act on them. Think of challenges as character building opportunities.

> *Hardships make or break people.*
> — Margaret Mitchell

## 8. Focus on What You Want and Like

To increase your chances of attracting prosperity and abundance, concentrate your efforts on doing things that fill you up with joy and the zest for life. Make a list of everything you find enjoyable and inspiring. Then in a second column, write down what you can begin to invest in those activities. This will give you the motivation to pursue your dreams with vigor and enthusiasm. This positive vibration of inspiration and enjoyment points you in the right direction for success.

> *Just don't give up trying to do what you really want to do. Where there is love and inspiration, I don't think you can go wrong.*
> — Ella Fitzgerald

9. **Dare to Change your Circumstances**

You have a choice in life to accept your financial position or change it. If you choose to plug along in life hoping that something will change for the better, you will not get very far. Remember that you always have the power of choice when it comes to changing your circumstances. As an example, women who are in jobs they don't enjoy often feel powerless and that there's nothing they can do. However, our life is a result of our choices, regardless of how difficult they may be. If the situation you find yourself in decreases the chances of success, it's up to you to change them.

*In America nobody says you have to keep the circumstances somebody else gives you.*
Amy Tan

10. **Have a Financial Plan**

Create a financial plan starting with how much you want to be earning and then work backwards. Include goals, benchmarks, things you want to have and the lifestyle you want to live. Have savings and investment goals and action plans for getting there. Focusing on the end result will keep you motivated to stick to your plan.

*It takes as much energy to wish as it does to plan.*
Eleanor Roosevelt

## 11. Accept Responsibility for Your Mistakes

Accept responsibility for mistakes or bad decisions. Pointing the finger of blame at other people or circumstances can blind you to the lessons you can learn. There is a saying: "Every master was once a disaster." Be willing to look squarely at your failures and ask "How can I do better next time?"

*In the long run, we shape our lives, and we shape ourselves. The process never ends until we die. And the choices we make are ultimately our own responsibility.*

Eleanor Roosevelt

## 12. Be Happy

You happiness does not depend on the size of your wallet or bank account. On the contrary, having a positive mind and a happy, upbeat attitude will help you attract the good things in life. Many studies have proven that a person living in a happy state generally gets much further in just about everything they do. Choose to have a happy, positive attitude. Just as a bad attitude can pull you down, a good attitude and a happy, healthy mind will make you magnetic to prosperity.

*Often people attempt to live their lives backwards; they try to have more things, or more money, in order to do more of what they want, so they will be happier. The way it actually works is the reverse. You must*

*first be who you really are, then do what you need to do, in order to have what you want.*
Margaret Young

## 13. No Shortcuts

Adopt as your own the motto "Anything worth doing is worth doing well." There are few shortcuts to success. Attracting money comes from giving value. Trying to get something for nothing usually results in getting nothing. Always strive for excellence and to do your best even if it requires a little more time and effort.

*It's definitely thrilling to know that you studied for something, and then you went in, and tried to do your best, and then somebody dug what you did.*
Paula Garces

## 14. Have Courage

Growing your money can be risky. Investing in new projects, creating business partnerships, and investing in our own personal development includes the risk of failure. However, there is no success without failure. Having courage means you are willing to take the risks, stick to your goals, and keep your commitment to yourself. Moving forward in spite of fear: this is the definition of courage.

*Life shrinks or expands in proportion to one's courage.*
Anais Nin

## 15. Enjoy Learning About How Money Works

To gain knowledge about a subject, one must take an active interest in learning and study. The best way to learn is to see the learning process as an enjoyable journey. Many people keep themselves from learning by expecting that they will be experts quickly and easily. This is not how learning works. Enjoy the process of discovery and always continue walking down the path of knowledge.

*I am not afraid of storms for I am learning how to sail my ship.*

Louisa May Alcott

## 16. Give Back

Share your wealth through donation to non-profits, charities or foundations that support those less fortunate than yourself. Even if you don't have much, there are always people that have less. Giving money away with planning and consistency sends a message to your mind that you have more than enough—the opposite of scarcity thinking—and that you expect to have more.

*Giving opens the way for receiving.*

Florence Scovel Shinn

## 17. Seek Input

Whatever your plan to create financial abundance, conduct "sanity checks" throughout the process of reaching your goal. This could be done with a coach, someone you trust or someone who has accomplished what you desire to accomplish. Ask for honest feedback about your plan and as you move forward, bounce concerns or new ideas off them to help keep you on the right track. Two heads are better than one and fresh eyes see double what one pair sees.

*All of us, at certain moments of our lives, need to take advice and to receive help from other people.*
Alexis Carrel

## 18. Beware of Toxic Poisoning

There will be people in your life who are jealous of your drive, goals or success. Your success may trigger their insecurities and they may try to tear you down or discourage you. If you are serious about reaching your financial goals and being successful, you will need to protect yourself from this negativity. While you may not be able to get these people out of your life completely, you should avoid them as much as possible. If you see any of these people every day, keep your goals to yourself, and talk about your dreams only with those who support you.

*When poison words are spoken by others do not swallow the poison.*
June Davidson

## 19. Be an Astute Observer

To learn how to attract financial abundance, observe those who are already doing it. Observe those who are failures. Can you see the difference? Then observe your own behaviors and the results that you get. Becoming an astute observer allows you to see what is hidden: this is where the secrets to success lie.

> *To acquire knowledge, one must study; but to acquire wisdom, one must observe.*
> Marilyn Vos Savant

## 20. Birds of a Feather Flock Together

If you have a goal of creating wealth, abundance, and financial security, find friends and mentors who either have achieved that same goal or who are also working towards their goals and dreams. It is important to surround yourself with people that can identify with your goal and passion, people who understand the burning desire to succeed and who are willing to encourage you. Jim Rohn said, "You are the average of the five people you spend the most time with." Avoid naysayers and downers!

> *Birds of a feather always stick together.*
> Anonymous

## 21. The Little Red Engine Who Could

Do you remember the story of the caboose that was desperately trying to make it over a very large hill? He kept telling himself repeatedly, "I think I can, I think I can." When you start feeling overwhelmed or defeated, tell yourself aloud these same words. Create positive affirmations to carry with you and repeat them during the day. Write them out first thing in the morning and last thing at night. Just thinking about something doesn't make it happen so you need to take appropriate action. The voice you have in your head will determine your success or defeat. Having these positive words in your head will bolster your belief that you can do whatever you think you can.

*Don't get in stuck in start.*

June Davidson

## 22. Be Proactive

Develop the habit of tackling problems before they arise. It's easy to put things off that are uncomfortable or challenging but doing exactly that strengthens your proactivity muscle! Be proactive especially with your financial concerns as this can save you money and precious time.

*Footprints in the sands of time are not made by sitting down.*

Anonymous

## 23. Stay Motivated

When striving for financial success and a feeling of security, it is critical to stay motivated. Fill your mind daily with inspiring and motivational material from seminars, books, movies and audio programs, especially when doubts and negativity creep in. A few excellent motivators include Suze Orman, Iyanla Vanzant, Louise Hay, Barbara De Angelis, Martha Stewart, Jim Rohn and Les Brown.

> *No woman can control her destiny if she doesn't give to herself as much as she gives of herself.*
> 
> Suze Orman

## 24. Cut Yourself Some Slack

Determination, commitment and dedication are essential for success. However, avoid being so hard and critical with yourself that the journey to success becomes misery. Beating yourself up is a waste of time. You will make mistakes. Learn from them. Allow yourself some room to risk and fail. You will then have more information on how to succeed. When you fall, pick yourself up and then get back to business.

> *It is impossible to live without failing at something, unless you live so cautiously that you might as well not have lived at all, in which case you have failed by default.*
> 
> J.K. Rowlings

## 25. Be Passionate

Fall in love with the idea of your success. Cultivate a passion for achievement, goal realization, and continuous growth. You may not be passionate about making money, but you can be passionate about what you can do with it: donations, helping family, college fund for your kids. By having passion for what you are doing and driving towards it, you will automatically put more effort into it.

> *Every great dream begins with a dreamer. Always remember, you have within you the strength, the patience, and the passion to reach for the stars to change the world.*
> — Harriet Tubman

## 26. Don't Settle for Less Than What is Possible for You

If you know that you have the talents, skills and abilities to achieve great wealth and prosperity, why settle for just getting by? The difference in effort and time to go from mediocre to excellence is not that great. Set your sights high and have a little faith that you can become all you can be.

> *Sometimes it takes a heartbreak to shake us awake & help us see we are worth so much more than we're settling for.*
> — Mandy Hale

## 27. Release the Fear of Failure

It's normal to not want to fail. However, anyone with any measure of success has failed repeatedly because to strive for success means that you will fail. The seed of success lies in every failure. How well you deal with failure and how much you learn from it is the determining factor between struggle and positive expectation that attracts prosperity. Set realistic goals and adjust, revisit, or change when necessary.

> *You may encounter many defeats, but you must not be defeated. In fact, it may be necessary to encounter the defeats, so you can know who you are, what you can rise from, how you can still come out of it.*
>
> Maya Angelou

## 28. No Excuses

J.K Rowling, author of the Harry Potter books, was a single mother on state welfare. Singer Joni Mitchell had polio and had to give her daughter up for adoption. Painter Joni Erickson was paralyzed from the neck down yet learned to paint with her mouth. Today, her paintings are famous around the world and worth millions. You may have to make adjustments from time to time to deal with challenges, but don't make excuses for not exchanging your unique talents for wealth and abundance. Believe that there is a way!

> *I attribute my success to this— I never gave or took any excuse.*
>
> Florence Nightingale

## 29. Learn Patience

Accumulating wealth and creating an abundant mindset takes time. Any goal worth setting will require time and effort. Oftentimes, things must happen in their own time. Be patient with yourself, the people around you, and the process it takes to achieve your goals. This is what is referred to as "paying your dues." This includes setbacks, obstacles, failures and changing strategies. Keep moving forward with determination and your patience will be rewarded.

> *Patience is not simply the ability to wait—it's how we behave while we're waiting.*
> — Joyce Meyer

## 30. Practice Effective Time and Resource Management

Those that create success and attract wealth know the value of their time and energy. They know how to stick to a schedule. The are aware of how and when to use their time, money and energy resources at the best time in the best way. Learn how to do this and you will learn how to do more with less.

> *You can't make up for lost time. You can only do better in the future.*
> — Ashley Ormon

**31. Make Opportunities**

Sitting and waiting for opportunities to come to you may result in a few, but going out looking for them will harvest you an abundant return. Rather than wait for opportunity to find you, you must create them. People that have reached a wealthy financial status will tell you that they look for ways to seize opportunities, not wait for opportunities to come knocking on their door.

*Life is an opportunity, benefit from it.*
                                                    Mother Theresa

**32. Attitude**

Attempting to create wealth for yourself and your family will not be easy. There will be challenges, disappointments and obstacles. Having the right attitude is essential for your success. A good attitude will allow you to turn any bad situation into a learning experience. You have heard the saying; "The glass is either half-full or half-empty." Having this attitude will allow you to see opportunities that you will miss with a bad attitude. The result is that you will feel better, have more energy, and have greater opportunities for success.

*The key to life is your attitude. Whether you're single or married or have kids or don't have kids, it's how you look at your life, what you make of it. It's about making the best of your life wherever you are in life.*
                                                    Candace Bushnell

33. **Have an Attitude of Gratitude**

Be thankful for everything; for your whole life, for your accomplishments and for your failures. Even if you are not where you want to be financially, be grateful for what you do have. If you live in the U.S. and have running water and plumbing, you have more than most of the world does. Appreciation goes a long way towards attracting prosperity.

> *"Thank you" is the best prayer that anyone could say. I say that one a lot. Thank you expresses extreme gratitude, humility, understanding.*
> Alice Walker

34. **Keep a Journal**

As you work to create a mindset of abundance and prosperity, it can be helpful to keep your thoughts in a journal. This not only allows you to vent frustrations and negativity, but also allows you to write down your goals, your growth and what you've learned. Putting your thoughts down on paper allows you to see them more clearly. Start a journal and track everything you have accomplished. Go back and see how you have progressed and grown.

> *Whether you're keeping a journal or writing as a meditation, it's the same thing. What's important is you're having a relationship with your mind.*
> Natalie Goldberg

## 35. Reward Yourself

When we are children we are given rewards for desired behavior. When people do well in their job, they get raises. As you accomplish your goals, reward yourself. Create positive associations with accomplishments by treating yourself. Set money aside for your rewards.

*Notice the small things. The rewards are inversely proportional.*

Liz Vassey

## 36. Keep Your Eyes Open for Scams

It's an unfortunate fact of life that there are people who will try to cheat you, lie to you and defraud you. If something appears too good to be true IT IS! Due diligence and thorough research are required before jumping into an opportunity that promises unusually lucrative returns for little risk. If someone is pushy, wanting you to make a quick decision on any type of investment, do not walk away – RUN away!

*Buyer Beware!*

Anonymous

## 37. See the Big Picture

As you work on increasing your financial abundance and begin to attract more opportunities for wealth, there will be many challenges, both big and small, that can distract your energy and focus. Be sure you are not "majoring in minor things" by picking your battles wisely. Keep your eye on the ultimate goal, and avoid wasting precious time and energy on menial matters that can clutter your mind and dilute your focus.

*One never notices what has been done;*
*one can only see what remains to be done.*
— Marie Currie

## 38. Make the Best of Each Day

Each day, we are given a few precious hours to create our lives. Yesterday is gone and tomorrow is promised to no one. Live each day as though it were your last and make the most of those few hours. They can be used to make a difference in your life or the lives of others. Even if it is something small, every baby step adds up to a huge success in the end.

*Every day is a new day, and you'll never be able to*
*find happiness if you don't move on.*
— Carrie Underwood

## 39. Make the Process an Adventure

What if life is just one big adventure? What if it's all about seeing what you can do with time, a body and a mind? See your journey as an exciting adventure. Attempt to recapture the sense of wonder and magic that you had as a child. Carry this sense of wonder and excitement with you as you strive towards achieving your prosperity goals.

*Life is either a daring adventure or nothing.*
Helen Keller

## 40. Avoid Neglecting The Things That Matter

Sometimes things that seem small and insignificant can have a huge impact on your business or finances. Letting these things slip through the cracks can cost you time and money. Little things can quickly add up and become a costly big mess if not taken care of in a timely and efficient manner. Like a fruit tree, what you neglect will wither. Your growing abundance requires time and attention to detail to provide you a bountiful harvest.

*More business is lost every year through neglect than through any other cause.*
Rose Kennedy

## 41. Offer Praise

No one does it alone. You will have people helping you, either as employees, mentors, or friends and family. Make it a point to always express appreciation and praise. These people are an important part of your success and by showing your gratitude towards them, they will show dedication and work hard to help you reach your goal. Give praise in the company of others and offer constructive criticism in private. Reinforce praise with rewards such as certificates, trophies or small gifts. It has been proven that people will work harder for an award or a title than they will for an increase in pay.

*Sandwich every bit of criticism between two layers of praise.*
— Mary Kay Ash

## 42. Set Daily Goals

There's a saying: "Success by the inch is a cinch, by the yard it's very hard." Great things are built one piece at a time. Setting daily goals allows you to add a few pieces each day in an organized and effective manner. A goal can be as simple as a follow up phone call or email. The key is to schedule it and get it done so that you can feel good about what you have accomplished.

*I cannot do everything, but I can do something. I must not fail to do the something that I can do.*
— Helen Keller

## 43. Collaborate with Others

No one has all the knowledge or resources necessary to achieve their goals. Some of what you need will have to come from other people. Network and find other successful people who you can partner with in a mutually beneficial way. These relationships can help you answer questions, provide guidance, and provide the ongoing support and encouragement you will need. Remember that two heads are better than one.

*Alone we can do so little. Together we can do so much.*
Helen Keller

## 44. Nurture Relationships with Clients and Partners

Communicate often with your clients and partners. If there is an issue or problem, show them the respect they deserve and resolve the issue quickly. Send cards, make phone calls and connect through email. This will let your clients know that you are there for them and care about their success. Your clients and partners are your link to success and the difference you make in their lives will touch more than just those individuals. Be willing to go above and beyond for them.

*As you navigate through your life, be open to collaboration. Other people and other people's ideas are often better than your own. Find a group of people who challenge and inspire you, spend a lot of time with them, and it will change your life.*
Amy Poehler

## 45. Repositioning and Reflection

Take time regularly to reflect on what you have accomplished and milestones yet to be reached to ensure you are still heading in the right direction. Adjustment and repositioning along the way to wealth is perfectly normal and expected. If there are ongoing struggles or negativity, try to identify changes that can make it better. Don't continue to battle this issue; reflect on what hasn't been working, and reposition yourself to avoid unnecessary frustration and aggravation.

> *Attach yourself to your passions, but not to your pain. Adversity is your best friend on the path to success.* — Unknown

## 46. Accept Responsibility

You and you alone are responsible for the level of wealth and prosperity you attract. You may have help or you may be hindered, but how you respond is up to you. Surround yourself with the right people, collaborate when you can, but avoid blaming others for the choices you have made. You are the captain of your ship, guide it carefully and thoughtfully, and should you find yourself in dangerous waters, be ready to make the tough choices about what to do.

> *I believe that we are solely responsible for our choices, and we have to accept the consequences of every deed, word, and thought throughout our lifetime.*
> — Elisabeth Kubler-Ross

## 47. Share Your Abundance

If you have been gifted with prosperity and abundance, share it with those less fortunate. Money likes to flow. Hold it too tight and the flow will dry up. This is why almost all who are happy millionaires donate their time, money and energy to charities and causes that help others. If you can't donate money, then donate time as a volunteer. In addition, you never know who you might meet that will help you on your road to prosperity and abundance.

*For it is in giving that we receive.*
                                                            Francis of Assisi

## 48. Record Keeping

Like anything of value, your money needs attention. Know what your money is doing and where it's going by keeping accurate and up to date records. This would include contact information, investor information, business plans, attorney information, and accounting and bookkeeping. Be sure to back up your computer files. Be organized so that you can find what you need quickly. Hire someone to help you if needed.

*Manage and keep track of your own money because the Universe has trusted you with it.*
                                                              June Davidson

## 49.  Get Out of Debt

Work diligently to pay off your debt, especially credit card debt that will cost you a fortune in interest. This is especially important if you will be seeking funding to create wealth. The amount of debt you have in relation to your income affects your ability to borrow money needed for investment or growth. Before applying for a loan or making a presentation to an investor to ask for money, make sure that your records and credit are clean.

> *If you have debt I'm willing to bet that general clutter is a problem for you too.*
> — Suze Orman

## 50.  Read, Read, Read

Read to educate yourself and stay current in your area of expertise as well as studying wealth creation and wealth management. Read about current trends, company failures or successes, new ideas and new technology for managing money. We live in the age of information at your fingertips. Seek out the information that will be helpful to you and use it.

> *The book you don't read won't help you.*
> — Jim Rohn

## 51. Location, Location, Location

Pay attention to the environment in which you work because the effect on your ability to attract prosperity can be significant. Does your work area contribute to your success or hinder it? Keep it clean, organized and free from clutter. Is your place of business inviting or is it scary? If it's not possible to move your business, then spruce it up with plants and decorative touches. If you are looking for a location to start a business, get a feeling for the location, get a sense of its energy. Do not settle for any location as a means of getting the doors of your business open. Instead, take the appropriate amount of time and find the "right" location. This will be one of the best decisions you can make.

> *Where ever you go, there you are. So make sure that wherever you go is where you want to be.*
> — Ted A. Moreno

## 52. Good Habits

Good habits are essential for success in any endeavor. Good habits include discipline, organization, time management, dressing for success, personal hygiene, study and education. Good habits mean daily consistent action towards your goal. Master your habits, or you will be a slave to them.

> *Creativity is a habit, and the best creativity is the result of good work habits.*
> — Twyla Tharp

## 53. ICAN: Improvement, Constant and Never Ending

Always seek to improve. Avoid thinking that you have all the answers and that there is nothing more for you to learn. Nothing can bring you down more quickly than this type of blind arrogance. Accept the fact that you do not have all the answers and more importantly, be open and listen to recommendations from other people. You never know when someone will have an idea that will make things easier and more functional; ultimately helping you arrive at your prosperity goals more efficiently.

*The mind is like a parachute- it works only when it is open.*

Anonymous

## 54. When You Think It, Ink it

Keep a journal or notepad handy. Million dollar ideas are available at all times, whether you are driving, washing dishes, taking a walk or just sitting and thinking. Don't allow a good idea to be forgotten; when you have an idea, write it down immediately. Keep your ideas and thoughts in a journal so that you can revisit them. Sometimes ideas come to fruition when they are ready. Plant them by writing them down so they have time to ripen.

*For me, writing something down was the only road out.*

Anne Tyler

## 55. Take Care of Yourself

To have the energy and mental acuity to create success and maintain it, you must take care of yourself, both physically and emotionally. Eat right, exercise, and get adequate rest and relaxation. Without proper self care, you can end up struggling and your business could feel the effects. You body is the vehicle that will take you down the road to success. Keep it well maintained so that you can enjoy prosperous health and energy.

> *Nourishing yourself in a way that helps you blossom in the direction you want to go is attainable, and you are worth the effort.*
>
> — Deborah Day

## 56. Take Good Notes

When attending seminars, conferences or classes, be sure to take good notes. Research shows that you will only retain so much information by just listening but you will retain much more by taking notes. This is not always a natural skill but something that has to be acquired. Even if there are materials being handed out, scribble something down if it strikes you. Good notes will help you learn better and provide additional reference points.

> *Talk does not cook rice so cook rice and take notes.*
>
> — Chinese Proverb

## 57. Participate

Another way to get more value out of seminars, lectures and classes is to participate by asking questions or making valid points. Participation is a great way to remember what is being taught and it can give you visibility to get your views across and let others know and see your skills and capabilities.

> *Too many women in too many countries speak the same language of silence.*
> — Hillary Clinton

## 58. Be Serious

Take your efforts to attract wealth and prosperity seriously. Success is a serious thing and it takes serious dedication. Have the mindset that this is not going to be all fun or play, at least not in the beginning.

> *All serious daring starts from within.*
> — Eudora Welty

## 59. Study Your Craft

Whether your goal is to accumulate wealth, be the best in your profession, or to develop personally, you must set aside some time to study your craft. Whatever your goal, take time to read, research, and ask questions. Free educational resources, such as the public library, are plentiful in this information age and can grant you any information you seek. Even a few minutes of study a day can make a difference in how high you can fly.

> *You have got to pay attention, you have got to study and you have to do your homework. You have to score higher than everybody else. Otherwise, there is always somebody there waiting to take your place.*
> 
> Daisy Fuentes

## 60. Apply What You Learn

Reading, studying and researching are a good start. However, information by itself is useless unless it is applied. Apply what you have learned through each phase of the process of reaching your financial goals. It is in the doing that our knowledge become power.

> *You'll get younger not from what you read but from what you apply in your life.*
> 
> Victoria Moran

## 61. Provide Yourself Leisure Time

A life of prosperity and abundance means that you allow yourself some time for pleasure and leisure. Being successful through goal achievement is hard work, so to avoid burnout, you need to treat yourself to a night out or just time to sit back, read, watch TV, and do absolutely nothing once in awhile. Even God took a day off.

> *I believe in manicures. I believe in overdressing. I believe in primping at leisure and wearing lipstick. I believe in pink. I believe happy girls are the prettiest girls. I believe that tomorrow is another day, and... I believe in miracles.*
>
> Audrey Hepburn

## 62. Set Realistic Goals

Set yourself up for success by setting goals that are realistic and achievable. Trying for results overnight can result in fatigue, disappointment and discouragement. Do an analysis to determine a realistic time frame to reach your specific financial or personal goals. Otherwise, you may become frustrated and quit!

> *Being in control of your life and having realistic expectations about your day-to-day challenges are the keys to stress management, which is perhaps the most important ingredient to living a happy, healthy and rewarding life.*
>
> Marilu Henner

## 63. Express Your Goals, Dreams and Desires

Find people you trust to share your dreams of financial security and stability. This keeps the goal in front of your mind and maintains your level of excitement. Furthermore, you may find people willing to help you. Those people are going to be expecting, and happy, to see you succeed. By talking about your goals, you are creating a motivational system of accountability.

> *Never dull your shine for somebody else.*
> — Tyra Banks

## 64. Don't Make Hasty Decisions

Avoid making financial decisions when under extreme pressure or emotion. If at all possible, acquire information or at least the input of someone knowledgeable. If you can, avoid making a decision until you have all the facts and/or have put a good amount of thought into it.

> *The key to good decision making is evaluating the available information — the data — and combining it with your own estimates of pluses and minuses. As an economist, I do this every day.*
> — Emily Oster

## 65. Learn to Manage Stress

Stress is inevitable. The only people without stress are in the graveyard. When you strive to play a bigger game and reach for audacious goals, you will encounter a fair amount of stress. However, overwhelming stress for long periods of time can be counterproductive and result in burnout and ill health. Learn to manage your stress. You can listen to relaxing tapes, get a professional massage, take a walk, or whatever helps you to relax. Be aware of when stress is stealing your fire.

> *My body needs laughter as much as it needs tears.*
> *Both are cleansers of stress.*
> Mahogany SilverRain

## 66. Learn How to Delegate

As you take on more responsibility and become more productive in building wealth, you will find that there are many more things to do than hours in the day. Your dream is only as big as your team. Don't be afraid to invest in other people's talents and skills by hiring people to handle bookkeeping, scheduling, phone calls, etc. You will be amazed at how much this will help ease the situation and allow you the proper amount of time to focus on the things that need your full attention.

> *The first rule of management is delegation. Don't try and do everything yourself because you can't.*
> Anthea Turner

## 67. Be a Problem Solver

Perhaps one of the greatest skills one can learn to attract money and prosperity is to get good at solving problems. See yourself as being bigger than your problems. When problems arise, as they will, take a few minutes to have whatever emotional reaction you need to have, then start solving the problem. Successful people trust in their ability to deal with problems effectively.

*The only way you will ever permanently take control of your financial life is to dig deep and fix the root problem.*
Suze Orman

## 68. Do Your Research

It is important to know what you are getting into. Conduct research into the business, industry, or interest associated with your particular financial goals. Research also helps you stay up to date on current trends and technology. Most importantly, knowing all the information that you can acquire can save you from serious mistakes costing time, energy and money.

*Research is formalized curiosity. It is poking and prying with a purpose.*
Zora Neale Hurston

## 69. Offer a Guarantee

Providing an ironclad guarantee is one of the best ways to add value to your service, product or time investment. If you borrow money, don't be afraid to put up a guarantee by securing the loan. If you have money that you owe, set a date of guaranteed payment. Make your word your bond.

> *I have friends and family that are filled with massive amounts of integrity. And it shouldn't be an oddity.*
> Sandra Bullock

## 70. Get Excited

Generate excitement and enthusiasm for your financial goals! Remember the excitement of your first prom or of the first time you rode a bike. Intention plus emotion plus action is the formula for attracting what you desire into your life, whether it's accomplishment, money or love. Remember some of the things that brought true excitement to your heart when you were growing up and add that same enthusiasm to your grownup life. Remember that the definition of enthusiasm is "the god within".

> *Don't you long for something different to happen, something so exciting and new it carries you along with it like a great tide, something that lets your life blaze and burn so the whole world can see it?*
> Juliet Marillier

## 71. Expand your Mind

What you accomplish in life will depend on your belief system. Whatever you believe you can accomplish, you will with the proper action. If you don't believe, you won't even try. Challenge your own beliefs about what is possible for you. Stretch your mind and reach just one-step higher than you thought you could reach. There are possibilities you can't even imagine. Begin to imagine them today.

> *Rule your mind or it will rule you.*
> — Anonymous

## 72. Learn to Lead

Learn to be a good leader, starting with leading yourself into productivity and accomplishment. So many people are looking for someone to lead them; if you have the opportunity, step up. Enjoy making a difference by guiding others to achieve their potential as well. This could be in your family, in your community and in your networking groups. Help people reach new horizons and in so doing you will fulfill your dreams.

> *Women are leaders everywhere you look, from a CEO to a housewife that holds together a home. Our country was built by women who stand alone.*
> — Denise Clark

## 73. Use Your Gift of Logic

Logic is simply thinking about a situation from all angles. Learn to use your analytical abilities to solve problems and find creative solutions. So many people simply do not want to think. Use your brain and this will put you head and shoulders about the others. Put aside emotion and think clearly and honestly.

> *We are afraid of ideas, of experimenting, of change.*
> *We shrink from thinking a problem through to a*
> *logical conclusion.*
> — Anne Sullivan

## 74. Give 100% Effort

Develop the habit and discipline of always giving 100% effort. Many people quit just before success because they got used to quitting before the finish line. You must train yourself to rise to challenges and not quit, especially when money is tight. You have to plan to go the extra mile and make personal sacrifices. Success requires giving 100% effort. Resolve to do no less.

> *It is with many enterprises as with striking fire; we*
> *do not meet with success except by reiterated efforts,*
> *and often at the instant when we despaired of success.*
> — Madame de Maintenon

## 75. Always Continue to Educate Yourself

The quest for knowledge and learning is never ending. Take some classes at your local college or community college in finance, accounting or business. Enhancing yourself on a personal level will boost everything about you, making you feel better, increasing your confidence and enabling you to achieve more. Consider also taking classes in an outside interest such as meditation, First Aid, or a computer class. Keep your learning muscle strong.

> *Real education should educate us out of self into something far finer—into a selflessness which links us with all humanity. Political education should do the same.*
>
> Nancy Astor

## 76. Understand your Objectives

Be very clear about your goals. Understand clearly not only why you want to attract wealth, but how. Study the biographies of those who have created or attracted abundance against great odds. Understand what it will take and what you must do when you get there. Take your knowledge and experience from the learning process to position yourself as the expert in the field.

> *The secret of joy in work is contained in one word—excellence. To know how to do something well is to enjoy it.*
>
> Pearl S. Buck

## 77. Raise Your Standards

You will get what you expect, especially from yourself. What would happen if you expected 5 or 10 percent more from yourself? You could increase your income 10 to 15 thousand dollars. Try raising the bar just a little bit and see what happens. Don't beat yourself up if you don't hit that extra bar, just continue to strive for more.

*Shoot for the moon and even if you miss, you'll land among the stars.* — Norman Vincent Peale

## 78. Tap into the Power of Your Subconscious Mind

The subconscious mind is a very powerful tool and makes up 88% of your mind power. Often, our minds are programmed to expect lack and are resigned to accept less prosperity that we can create. Take advantage of your subconscious mind by taking some time to pose questions to yourself and then allow your mind to hash them out while you sleep. In addition, give yourself positive affirmations right before bed as your subconscious mind is more open to them at that time.

*You will be a failure, until you impress the subconscious with the conviction you are a success. This is done by making an affirmation which clicks.* — Florence Scovel Shinn

## 79. Paint a Picture

Imagery is the language of the subconscious mind. If you want to impress new goals onto your mind, practice seeing them having been achieved. If your goal is to buy a new car, go to the dealership, have your picture taken in the car, then look at it daily. If your goal is to live in a nice house, get a clear image of what that house would look like. Seeing is believing! Paint a wonderful picture in your mind of what you desire in life. You can create a vision board by cutting pictures from magazines and arranging them as a vision of how you see your desired life.

*To achieve the impossible, one must think the absurd; to look where everyone else has looked, but to see what no one else has seen.*
Anonymous

## 80. Develop Consistency

Strive to keep your energies and time focused on your goals. Avoid being distracted by the "Shiny Object Syndrome" where you are distracted by new technology, trends, products etc. This will keep your efforts and focus steady and effective. The more you can stay the course the quicker you will reach your financial and business goals.

*The minute you settle for less than you deserve, you get even less than you settled for.*
Maureen Dowd

## 81. Just Do It

You've heard the phrase that Nike made famous. Most people don't achieve financial independence because they are not able or willing to take action. Procrastination can keep you stuck and miserable. Only you have the power to stop putting things off and just do it. The most important thing is to get started. Schedule your task as an appointment with yourself. You cannot reach second base unless you are willing to take your foot off first base.

> *Getting organized in the normal routines of life and finishing little projects you've started is an important first step toward realizing larger goals. If you can't get a handle on the small things, how will you ever get it together to focus on the big things?*
> — Joyce Meyer

## 82. Identify Procrastination Patterns

If procrastination holds you back from taking the steps you need to take to accrue wealth and prosperity, take time to study and get to know your own procrastination. Make a list of the things that stop you, such as fear or distractions. Identify when you are most prone to procrastinating. This will help you identify potential blocks so you can make the appropriate adjustments. Get clear about what is holding you back.

> *Procrastination has a tendency to lead to poverty.*
> — June Davidson

## 83. Want Versus Need

Develop a desire to create abundance and prosperity. Be motivated by the lifestyle you want to lead. Although fear and need are great motivators, the stress that comes from needing money can create negative energy. When you want something, it brings about intention, desire, and action. However, when you desperately need something, it can lead to pain, stress, and frustration.

*Learn to hide your need and show your skill.*

Jim Rohn

## 84. Be Independent

There will be pressure to conform to what is expected of you or to how other people think you be. You will encounter people that want to tell you how to think, what to do and what to believe. However, always stay connected to your own truth. Do what is right for you. This is your life, be independent of the pressure to conform as well as the expectations and opinions of others. Take control of your own destiny and emotional state. After proper consideration, stand firm in what you believe and refuse to be swayed or stopped by the opinions or beliefs of others.

*I am no bird and no net ensnares me: I am a free human being with an independent will.*

Charlotte Bronte

## 85. Economic Value

Seriously consider the opportunity that your talents skill and abilities afford you. What assets do you have that you can use to attract money, wealth and opportunity? There may be economic value in your ability to lead or organize. You may have space that you can rent or lease. Look around and see what needs your community or business has that are not being met and explore how you can meet those needs.

> *The most common way people give up their power is by thinking they don't have any.*
> — Alice Walker

## 86. Learn a New Skill

Make it a point to be always learning new skills that will enhance your ability to create and attract money. Learn to negotiate, or speak another language, or how to balance your checkbook or analyze a business deal. Make it a goal to learn a new skill every year and watch your income grow.

> *Learning how to learn is one of the most important skills in life.*
> — Nourma F. Fauziyah

## 87. Appreciate Everything in Your Life

Don't assume that you know what everything means. Don't presume to know why things work out the way they do. Many times, what seems to be a huge problem or even a catastrophe turns out to be a blessing in disguise. This is your path. Have a sense of deep gratitude for the opportunity to experience your life in all of its forms, for what it is and for what it is not. Appreciate everything. Learn as much as you can from every person you meet. You never know who will be your next teacher. The people you want to turn away may be the very people that come to your rescue when you are alone and adrift.

> *My parents are the coolest of the cool on every single level, and it's because they have a deep appreciation for every moment of their lives.*
>
> Rashida Jones

## 88. Diversify Your Wealth Attraction Efforts

Waiting to win the lottery is not a viable way to create wealth. Neither is focusing on one income stream or investment. The more ways you attract wealth, the more wealth you will have. A combination of passive income, investments, online marketing, and offering various services is much more likely to get you the financial security you desire.

> *Thoughtful financial planning can easily take a backseat to daily life.*
>
> Suze Orman

## 89. Believe In You

If you don't have the belief that you can achieve your desires, then you must create the belief. If you have any doubts about your ability and potential to live in abundance, realize that they are the result of old beliefs that were learned in the past. What was learned can be unlearned, and you can learn something new. Work daily to increase your confidence in the fact that you will achieve your dreams. It all starts with your belief in you.

> *Believe in yourself, take on your challenges, dig deep within yourself to conquer fears. Never let anyone bring you down. You've got to keep going.*
> — Chantal Sutherland

## 90. Know Your Most Profitable Activity

Take time to examine everything you do that brings you income and attracts wealth into your life. There are probably many things you do in your job or business, but not all of them are equally effective at creating wealth. Focus your time and energy on the most profitable activities. Remember the 80/20 rule: 20% of what you do will bring you 80% of your income.

> *I am a big believer that orderliness begets wealth.*
> — Suze Orman

## 91. Plan Your Costs

It is imperative to have a clear idea of what your monthly expenses are and to plan and budget accordingly. To get to where you want to be financially, you need to know exactly what your income must be and how that income will be produced. Don't wing it on a hope and prayer when it comes to your financial future. Do the numbers and project what you will need to live the way you want. Know your numbers and make sure they are accurate.

*Budgeting has only one rule: Do not go over budget.*
— Leslie Tayne

## 92. Timing is Everything

So much of your success in creating wealth and abundance will have to do with timing. Timing is everything. There is a right and a wrong time to start a business. There is a right and a wrong time to negotiate. There is a right and a wrong time to ask for a raise. There is a right and a wrong time to buy. There are two rules here: he who hesitates is lost and look before you leap. Timing is about knowing which adage to follow. Get help, ask advice, do research and think about the timing of your actions.

*I'm such a profound believer that timing is everything; I would tattoo that on my arm.*
— Drew Barrymore

## 93. Keep it Lean

The message to accumulate, consume, and spend beyond our means is a prevailing message in media and advertising. The desire to purchase the next shiny new object can be hard to resist. Furthermore, "retail therapy" or the tendency to buy things to feel good, can be counterproductive to our efforts to create abundance. Consider that real wealth is not how much you make but how much you keep. Work on improving the bottom line before you add more expenses to your business or lifestyle.

> *I continue to be drawn to clarity and simplicity. 'Less is more' remains my mantra.*
>
> Stephane Rolland

## 94. Get the Word Out

Whatever actions you are taking to increase the level of wealth and abundance in your life, be sure to share it with people that will support you. Whether it's a business endeavor, project, class or seminar, share it with others that will encourage you. You may decide to go to networking events, or speak at gatherings or write a blog. Whatever you do, if people need to hear about it, make sure you get the message out there.

> *There is a vitality, a life force, an energy, a quickening that is translated through you into action, and because there is only one of you in all time, this*

*expression is unique. And if you block it, it will never exist through any other medium and will be lost.*
Martha Graham

## 95. Keep Your Emotions in Check

Things go wrong sometimes. People don't meet your expectations. That check that's supposed to be in the mail fails to appear. At these times there's a tendency to to lose our cool. Learning to keep your emotions in check is not always an easy task. These times of disappointment will require you to react with integrity. You may feel like crying and feel as though your world has just ended. Keep telling yourself that it has not ended and you will just have to make some adjustments in your plan. Never allow your unchecked emotions to alienate an ally or partner, or allow you to do or say something you may regret.

*Life goes by fast. Enjoy it. Calm down. It's all funny. Next. Everyone gets so upset about the wrong things.*
Joan Rivers

## 96. Play Nice

What you do comes back to you. Study after study has shown that people with pleasing personalities have an easier time reaching success. This is because we all want to be associated with nice people. No one really wants to deal with someone that is often ill tempered and in a foul mood. Being pleasing is not enough; in addition, be polite, show true interest, and have a great sense of humor.

> *Those old adages— you attract more with honey; do unto others— are true. You can get attention by being acerbic or mean or making a bizarre comment. But by being nice, being empathetic, building relationships and listening, people begin to recognize that you're thoughtful and respectful of their position.*
> Shelley Moore Capito

## 97. Break Bad Habits

Everybody has bad habits that they want to change. Habits, regardless of size or nature, can be exceptionally difficult to break. But it is possible. Begin by identifying which habits are the biggest obstacles to your success. Work on changing one habit at a time. For example, if your habit is to overspend when you go into a particular store, then make a plan to go into that store with only the amount of money you can spend, or better yet, practice going into the store and buying nothing. Make changing the habit a goal that you work on every day. Get the help of a coach or hypnotherapist.

> *A change in bad habits leads to a change in life.*
> Jenny Craig

## 98. Improve Efficiency

There are only so many hours in a day, days in a week, weeks in a year, and years in a life. Use the time you have to develop your potential to its fullest. Honor the time you have by using it wisely and efficiently. Avoid people and activities that waste your precious time. Develop ways to work quickly and with focus. Abundance does not find its way to those who are wasteful.

*I will be ruthless in cutting out waste, streamlining structures and improving efficiency.*
                                                    Theresa May

## 99. Strive for Balance in Your Life

When you first learned to ride a bike, you needed balance to keep the bike upright. Once you had balance, you could ride! It is the same when you strive for success. You have to find balance not only for yourself but also for others around you. Balance involves providing time away from work for pleasure, but also, working extra hours when required. Balance is also knowing when a new direction is required, or when to walk away from a project, business or person.

*A wise woman recognizes when her life is out of balance and summons the courage to act to correct it, she knows the meaning of true generosity, that happiness is the reward for a life lived in harmony, with courage and grace.*
                                                    Suze Orman

## 100. Have Fun

Perhaps our mission is to see what we can do with this life, to see what we can create. We must assume that we are not put here simply to work hard and suffer. We must enjoy life. If you look at some of the most successful women in the world such as Martha Stewart, Oprah Winfrey, or J.K. Rowlings , you will find common threads that run between all of them. First, they started with nothing; second, they are all multi-millionaires many times over, and third, they have fun. They enjoy life, the people around them, and even find enjoyment in the challenges. This is a crucial element for success. Plan time to have fun, laugh, and play. This is as essential to success as hard work. Without allowing yourself to enjoy life by engaging in pleasurable, healthy activities, you will burn out and possibly sabotage your success.

*The trick is to enjoy life. Don't wish away your days, waiting for better ones ahead.*
                                                    Marjorie Pay Hinckley

## 101. Face your Weaknesses

Your weaknesses are your opportunities for success. They are areas that you can focus on for the purpose of making them strong. To become financially successful you must learn to deal with your weaknesses. Identify the areas you need to improve on and then take action to turn your weaknesses into strengths. Make a game of it: list all of your perceived weaknesses and start working on them one by one. Don't shy away from identifying skills or talents that you lack. You may not be able to turn all your weaknesses into strengths, but you can learn new skills that offset any lack of talent. Don't even call them weaknesses, call them "areas waiting to be made strong!"

*I understand now that the vulnerability I've always felt is the greatest strength a person can have. You can't experience life without feeling life. What I've learned is that being vulnerable to somebody you love is not a weakness, it's a strength.*

Elisabeth Shue

The gratification that comes from successfully dreaming a dream, setting a goal, making a plan and reaping the rewards is unsurpassed. Don't be afraid to assert yourself, take risks and work hard, it won't kill you!

Use these tips as guidelines to first be happy, and then to strive for something great. Read a few tips every day. If an idea comes to you, write it down. Create a daily ritual of affirming that you can and will be successful!

Come to believe that you can affect the Universe with the powerful and creative combination of Intention and Action. There will be times when you won't know how you will achieve your goals, but don't worry; the "hows" are the domain of the Universe. All you need to is to develop a clear intention of what it is you want, then with an attitude of faith and positive expectation, take action and succeed!

## A SPECIAL OFFER ONLY FOR READERS OF THIS BOOK: RECEIVE FREE COACHING SESSIONS!

Reading a book, getting inspired, and acquiring information is a great way to get started on the road to success! However, it's only the first step. You must continually take daily, consistent action. However, the reason most people don't succeed is because taking action and moving ahead with your dream can be challenging, and scary. That's why a coach can make the difference between success and just getting by.

If you are serious about moving beyond what you think is possible for you, then consider taking advantage of this special offer: **Four *free* 30 minute coaching sessions worth $400. Get coached for free!**

Every successful person has had a mentor or coach to guide them to success. Why not you?

**To take advantage of this free offer, email Ted at <u>ted@tedthecoach.com</u> with subject Ready To Succeed! Ted will contact you within 48 hours to set up your free sessions. Thank you for reading this book!**

## ABOUT THE AUTHORS

**Biography of Ted A. Moreno, C.Ht.**

Ted A. Moreno is a Prosperity Coach, published author, educator and speaker. Ted works with professional women to guide them out of money anxiety and into greater levels of prosperity, wealth and abundance.

He is a Certified NLP Practitioner, as well as a Certified Hypnotherapist. With more than fifteen years of mastery in the art of motivating people to take action, he brings a lifetime of expertise in the fields of personal development and human potential.

Ted combines his life experiences and humor with his expertise in coaching to help his clients move past their limitations and explore what is possible for them and their lives. He teaches his proven techniques to women business professionals seeking greater levels of excellence, success, and financial abundance. In addition to being a published author, he is a sought-after speaker and educator, teaching classes and workshops on wealth attraction, motivation, self hypnosis, and goal achievement.

Ted's first book, *The Ultimate Guide to Letting Go of Negativity and Fear and Loving Life* is available on Amazon.com.

**Contact Ted A. Moreno**
Web: www.TedMoreno.com/TedtheCoach.com
Email: Ted@TedtheCoach.com

## Biography of June Davidson

June Davidson is President of the American Seminar Leaders Association (ASLA) and President of Coaching Firm International (CFI). As a master trainer, she writes curriculum and trains others to create their own seminar curriculum in their niche. Her teaching style is based on experiential, accelerated learning. At CFI she trains and certifies coaches with each coach having his or her own well-defined area, similar to the specialization in large law firms. Action coaches certified by CFI are thoroughly trained and equipped with unique tools, such as ATAP (Access the Truth Accelerate Your Process)™, and methods for rapid brain pattern interrupts. CFI's coaches are trained and supported to develop a thriving business.

She is a master at identifying the unique rich niche of those she trains. She is an internationally acclaimed marketing guru and excellent at strategies for getting sponsorship money.

June has closely partnered with Jim Rohn on workshops and seminars. She was featured in his book *Rising to the Top* and authored *Coaching the Millionaire Within* and *Marketing Your Coaching with Seminars.*

June teaches in the Masters program as an adjunct professor at the University of Bucharest, Romania. She is a member of the National Association of Professional Woman (NAPW) National Association of Female Executives (NAFE), on faculty at CEO Space, and hosts her own radio show *Coaches Corner*.

June has founded Woman Against Child Trafficking, a non-profit organization working in the United States. She is a platform speaker at major events and has won numerous awards. She was the recipient of the 2013 Social Entrepreneur of the Year Awards for enlightening and empowering woman of all ages. In 2011, she received the coveted Women of Excellence Award by NAFE.

June Davidson is a visionary who wants to help others succeed. Instead of asking "What's in it for me?", June's life has been spent asking, "What can I do for you?" and over the years she has made an impact on countless lives.

**Contact June Davidson to learn more:**
American Seminar Leaders Association (ASLA): asla.com
Coaching Firm International (CFI): www.coachingfirminternational.com
Email: June@asla.com
Phone: 626.791.1211

Made in the USA
Columbia, SC
02 January 2018